# Wildness Within

## EXPERIENCE THE POWER
## OF YOUR AUTHENTIC SELF

ROBERT E. WAGNER

*Wildness Within: Experience the Power of Your Authentic Self*

Robert E. Wagner
Wild Sacredness, LLC
Ashland, Oregon
www.wildsacredness.com

ISBN: 978-0-9863114-3-7

Second Edition

Printed in the United States of America
10 9 8 7 6 5 4 3 2

*For the brave souls who have the courage, perseverance,*
*and self love to become all that they were meant to be.*

"You have a unique message to deliver, a unique song to sing, a unique act of love to bestow. This message, this song, and this act of love have been entrusted exclusively to the one and only you."

~ John Powell

# Introduction

WELCOME TO AN ENCOUNTER WITH YOUR WILD, AUTHENTIC SELF! Any lasting transformation begins with looking within. Our journey toward passionate living must begin with learning to love and honor our wild, sacred selves, embracing tools that nourish our thoughts, our bodies and our deepest dreams.

How do we get in touch with that 'wild', instinctive self—the part of us that reflects our truest character, beyond all the roles we play in our lives? The essence of us that 'lights up' when we're doing what stirs our passion?

At Wild Sacredness, we recognize the importance of being fully present as we explore deeper and truer aspects of ourselves. The following three exercises in *Wildness Within* are the perfect place to begin your journey toward a passionate, purposeful life. They begin with culturing Self Love—stirring a profound connection with your surprising, unique, wonderful self, and recognizing in your cells that you are complete, whole and perfect exactly as you present yourself at this moment.

Next we'll move on to Self Awakening—waking up to our true potential and purpose. We'll invite feedback from aquaintances on our strengths and weaknesses, and we'll listen for the still voice in the background of our lives, reminding us what our gifts are. Self Awakening means looking directly at what's working and not working in our lives, and realizing that we do have a choice to act from who we are, and achieve what we deeply desire.

This brings us to Self Empowerment—gathering the strength and commitment to manifest what we came here to do. This step involves directly experiencing our own power and seeing our mission become actualized—so it's no longer an idea in our awareness but a reality being extended to our community. Self Empowerment is reclaiming and bringing forth our power and purpose, and this is accomplished in a dramatic way through participation in the Sacred Vision Quest. (For a complete description of the Sacred Vision Quest—purpose, details, FAQs— visit **www.wildsacredness.com**.) On the quest, you have the opportunity to gain a deeper understanding of your self and remove obstacles standing in the way of bringing forth your unique gifts and living with passion and presence. It is a truly transformative experience that marks a major shift in the way you will henceforth live your life.

From the initial exercise of 'Self Reflections' to the transformation brought about by the Sacred Vision Quest, the promise of Wildness Within is achieved.

# THE EXERCISES

"THE REAL VOYAGE OF DISCOVERY
CONSISTS NOT IN SEEKING NEW
LANDSCAPES BUT IN HAVING
NEW EYES."

~ MARCEL PROUST

# Self Reflections

Y OU MAY HAVE HEARD IT BEFORE—creating a successful relationship begins with loving yourself. And you may have nodded in agreement. But what does that really mean? How can you get to the point of really *feeling* that self love inside—not just affirming it mentally, but radiating that glow that comes from accepting and honoring yourself just as you are, in this moment?

If you're not the current star of your universe, it's time to turn the camera lens on YOU and rediscover the spark lying there. The following exercise is simple and extremely powerful. It's a technique that can be practiced daily to cast the light on who you are, so your reflection mirrors back the truth and the self love can begin to flow.

◆ All you need to begin this exercise is to bring conscious awareness to what you do every single morning—take a glimpse of yourself as you get ready to take your morning shower. Some of us just do a quick check-in with the mirror with averted eyes, and some may avoid looking altogether for fear of what they'll see! But I am asking you to take a good long look.

◆ What do you see? If you greet yourself with love and enthusiasm, that's great. Your self love juices are already flowing. But if you don't...if there's a hesitation, or a quick judgment that makes you feel not so great about yourself...hang in there with me.

◆ You have a choice here. You can tense up, sensing there are parts of yourself you just can't embrace because you see 'imperfection' there, and look away—or you can just stop and LOOK, hold that gaze for a moment. You might find something you really like about yourself, that you feel proud of. You may find things you wish were different.

◆ But just hold the gaze, just BE with your reflection. Breathe in that person in front of you, with slow gentle breaths–then let go. You'll find that by being with the reflection, looking yourself in the eye, it can seem as if you're meeting yourself for the first time. Who is this person? Drink yourself in, just as you are. If some judgments arise, then I invite you to drop in deeper to the feelings that lie underneath these judgments. You may experience feelings of sadness, shame, or even embarrassment. But don't worry, by sending love to those parts of yourself you find difficult to embrace you allow these negative feelings to be released, thereby allowing more room for self-acceptance.

◆ Doing this exercise every morning only requires you and a mirror. It will only take a few minutes, but you do need to be present and take an honest look. You will notice new things each time that you are pleased with—the rich color of your hair, the way your lips curl when you smile, the softness of your breasts, the physical build of your body, the smoothness or strength of your legs, maybe even a lively twinkle in your eyes. And those things that make you feel less in some way, that tell you you're not 'enough'? Shower them with heart-felt love.

If there are things you can change and wish to, go right ahead—like the style or color of your hair, or the strength of your body. But some things aren't going to change: like your height, or a few wrinkles, or maybe a birthmark or scar. These things are a part of who you are and want to be loved and accepted. This exercise is not about the pursuit of 'perfection' or grasping on to a youthful appearance. It's about gracefully surrendering to your uniqueness and recognizing the inner beauty that shines through.

As the self-discovery continues, magical shifts begin to occur. You'll start finding things to love about yourself that you never noticed before. And you'll soon find that you can love ALL of you, gently and naturally. As you become more familiar with the mysterious YOU, the wonderfully unique YOU, and accept the person reflected back at you, your appreciation for this most special being increases. It is transformational.

◆ Once you are comfortable and lovingly accepting the reflection of your body, then I invite you to explore the reflection of your inner world. This involves looking deeply into the reflection from your eyes (the window to your soul).

◆ As you gaze into your eyes, ask yourself the following questions. *Are my actions and behavior mirroring the kind of man or woman I want to be? Am I truthful in my interactions with others? Am I treating others in the way I would like to be treated?* If you find yourself shying away or hesitating, then just close your eyes for a moment and take a few deep breathes. You may have realized that your integrity is less than what you deem acceptable for yourself. You may recognize that you've been speaking ill of others, for instance, or that you've recently been dishonest with someone.

◆ Again, I invite you to drop in deeper to the feelings lying underneath these actions and behaviors. You may discover feelings of jealousy, anger, or even self-loathing. Once again, send love to these aspects of yourself so that these negative emotions can be released, thereby bringing more freedom to choose a more appropriate action.

This is where your life begins to change—in this small space, doing this exercise for a few minutes each morning. You're finding the gold, and it is going to bring you a life filled with wonder, meaningful relationships, and deep fulfillment.

The person reflected back to you in your mirror is the one with whom you have the most important relationship of your life—it's the person who's with you through thick and thin, from your first breath to your last. As you make the journey to embrace him or her completely, your days will be filled with beautiful self reflections!

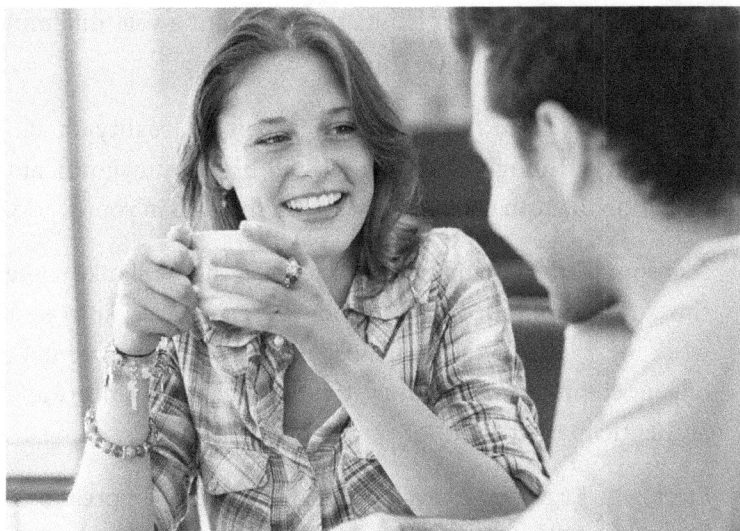

# Reflections from Others

I**T'S GREAT WHEN WE FEEL GOOD ABOUT OURSELVES,** when our self-esteem is high and we have a healthy self-confidence. But if some things aren't working as smoothly in our lives as they could be—if our business has taken a downward turn, or relationships aren't satisfying, or we don't have a romantic partner to share the good times with—maybe it's time to get some feedback from others.

Reflections from those who know us well are an invaluable asset. How do others see us? What are the dominant things that people notice when they're with us? Do their observations match how we think of ourselves, or is there a gap?

We do have control over how we are perceived, but first we need an accurate, unbiased picture of how we come across to others. We certainly don't want to steer people away with behaviors we aren't even aware of. In relationships, our best intentions may be derailed by attitudes or habits that send out a very different impression from the one we think we're sending.

So it's time to go to family and friends for a 'reality check.' This exercise, though challenging, will bring you significant information that can change the way you show up in your world.

◆ Ask some family members and friends if they will take some time, one-on-one, to chat about how they perceive you: in your work life, personal relationships, and generally as a member of your community. Encourage them to be honest, sincere and authentic in their sharing.

◆ Start by telling them you value their opinions and impressions. Show them that you're ready and willing to receive honest feedback. Let them know why you're asking: because you want to be as successful in all areas of your life as you can, and if there's anything in the way of that, you want to know so you can change or refine it.

◆ Encourage your family and friends to go deeper than superficial things, so you can get to the core of how you show up. You might want to prepare some questions of your own to get them going, like "If you were going on a long trip, would you want me in the car with you? Why or why not?" Or: "If you were in a crisis, would you call me up?" Or: "One thing I like about myself is.....do you think that is accurate? What do YOU like about me or think I'm good at?" Or: "I broke up with another girlfriend after a year, repeating a pattern I have..any idea what's going on, from your perspective?" This will indicate to them that you're ready to hear some honest feedback.

Be prepared for this to be edgy and challenging—you'll get the most out of it this way. I would suggest that you just be open to receiving feedback and not become defensive. If you find yourself getting triggered, just take a deep breath and continue to listen. Since you've been working with loving yourself more deeply with the Self Reflections exercise, you know how to incorporate some potentially unflattering feedback without it damaging your self love. Applaud yourself for the courage to see yourself from others' eyes!

Having yourself reflected back by others builds trust, self-confidence, integrity, flexibility, and keeps you aligned with your personal goals. Next thing you know, your friends and family will be asking you to do the same exercise and reflect back to them how they are showing up!

"WITHOUT REFLECTION, WE GO BLINDLY ON OUR WAY, CREATING MORE UNINTENDED CONSEQUENCES, AND FAILING TO ACHIEVE ANYTHING USEFUL."

~ MARGARET J. WHEATLEY

"In every walk with nature one receives far more than he seeks."

~ John Muir

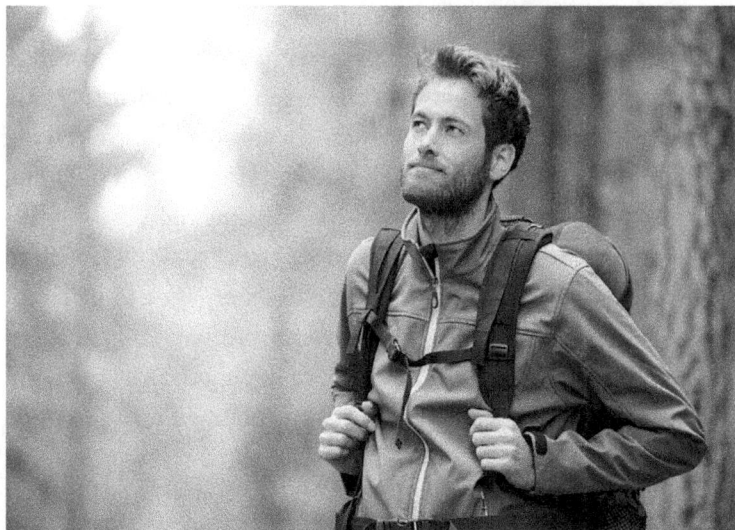

# Reflections from Nature

P EOPLE HAVE ALWAYS KNOWN THE VALUE of a good walk or a hike to a beautiful spot in nature when they're facing a turning point in their life, when challenges become overwhelming, or when their thoughts and direction are a bit muddled. What I'm presenting to you here contains that formula, but is even more effective and regenerating.

It's called a "Day Walk," or in Native American tradition, a "Medicine Walk." The insights and energy you'll gain from being immersed in nature and keenly observing your surroundings can provide healing ('medicine') for both mind and body. It's an intentional time, centered around being alone in the wilderness and sometimes fasting—although that's not required.

◆ You're simply going to take a hike, maybe for a half-day or a day, or as long as you like. Some begin at sunrise and end at sunset. Pick a place that won't have too many visitors, so you can sink into the silence more easily, walk at your own pace, sit for long periods, or even talk to yourself! A spot that pulls you in an unusual or mysterious way might be the right choice. Like all ceremonies, some preparation is necessary—you'll want to bring a daypack, adequate water and emergency food, a first aid kit, proper clothing for the expected weather. In other words, you want to be comfortable carrying things you might need, but you don't want to take so much you feel burdened down. Also, be sure to let a friend know where you're going and when you expect to return, in case something happens and you need assistance.

◆ The main point of this Day Walk is that it's about BEING, not DOING. It's a special opportunity to be alone in nature, and it's your ceremony, self-generated and self-directed. So make it fit your desire.

◆ Again, like all ceremonies, it has a beginning and an end. If I'm going on a Day Walk, I might begin at a trailhead and smudge myself. 'Smudging' is an ancient practice for cleansing a person's energy field, handed down from Native American tradition. You simply light a small bundle of sage and intentionally wave the smoke around your body. Swirl the smoke all around you, from head to toe; feel free to speak out or hold an intention as you do the smudging, such as "I cleanse my body, mind, and spirit in preparation for receiving the most from my Day Walk." Smudging draws forth the energies of sacred plants, restoring balance to one about to enter a sacred ceremony.

I also will do a blessing of the seven directions before I set out. This ritual, common to many cultures, calls on the directions to construct a sacred space for honoring your activity. This practice of addressing and revering the qualities represented by the directions is a way of giving thanks for one's blessings. For a downloadable PDF version of this blessing, go to **www.wildsacredness.com**, under *Sacred Vision Quests*.

◆ Next, I'll set my intention: It can be as simple as to savor this time, or to get some clarity on a particular issue I'm currently facing in my life. It can be to reflect on some event or come closer to someone in my life. Usually I draw a physical line in the dirt when I start my walk—from that point on, I'm in ceremony. During this special time, everything I encounter will be touched with sacred meaning. When I return and cross back over my line, I'm out of ceremony.

◆ This walk is a beautiful opportunity to drink in what nature has to offer, to listen to what you might hear. I'm asking nature for guidance. There's no place you have to GO, just be present as you stroll along. Walking slowly might heighten your senses and receptivity. Drop all agendas, and let your intention simmer, as you innocently experience whatever thoughts happen to come up. You don't need to try and analyze what's happening—it's enough that you've put your intention out there to the universe, which might respond to it in obvious or subtle ways. It's a good idea to bring a journal, to write down thoughts that seem meaningful or just to reflect on what is happening. You may notice specific animals or birds that seem to have something to say, or a particular view might trigger something deep inside. Follow it. You may begin to think of people you haven't thought of for years, whether they're living or have passed on.

Nature will mirror back to you situations or aspects of yourself or your life that need to be addressed—all you need to do is let them in, be aware of them. You'll soon find that the things you see, feel and hear can be full of symbolic meaning—ready to deliver realizations that can be simple, profound, and often unexpected.

Savor the moments as they unfold, in this wonderful opportunity to disengage from your daily life and drop into ceremony. Really enjoy the being, not the doing. You'll be pleasantly surprised at what nature reflects back to you.

I F YOU'VE FOUND THE INFORMATION in this booklet helpful and inspiring, then we invite you to learn more at: **www. wildsacredness.com**. Click on the "Wildness Within" offering to learn more about honoring yourself—and read about the transformative Sacred Vision Quest journey.

If these exercises have sparked you to go deeper, give Robert a call at 541-201-3411 or email robert@wildsacredness.com. He offers a **FREE "Reclaim Your Wild, Authentic Self" session**—where you can share the results from the exercises one-on-one with a qualified guide, and learn how the tools of Wild Sacredness can keep your momentum going to create an authentic, empowered life. The session will:

1. Create a clear picture of the authentic life you really want to have.

2. Uncover the building blocks for having the life of your dreams.

3. Discover the #1 thing blocking you from having your authentic life.

4. Identify the actions that will move you towards this goal.

5. Show you EXACTLY what to do next to create the passionate, authentic life you want—and deserve!

Robert is also available to give presentations and lively experiential workshops on awakening to your wild, authentic self, embracing self love, and gaining empowerment through the vision quest ceremony.

*Wild Sacredness is dedicated to bringing forth the authentic, passionate essence within each of us, and nurturing that as we manifest our individual power and purpose, our capacity for deep, intimate relationships, and a dynamic, engaged relationship with our community.*

## Robert E. Wagner
### Founder and Director, Wild Sacredness

WILD SACREDNESS is the outgrowth of the inner and outer journeying Robert has been doing for most of his life. As an Eagle Scout and member of the Order of the Arrow, he spent his first time alone in the wilderness as a young teen. Soon after that, he began his practice of Transcendental Meditation and spent many years living and studying in a prominent spiritual community.

In 1996, Robert participated in his first vision quest; he has continued to use the quest as a tool for empowerment and self-awareness, going on a vision quest every year. The discovery of Tantra as a vehicle for profound healing and fulfillment fit perfectly into Robert's array of tools for embracing one's wild, sacred, sensual presence and sharing that with others. As a member of the Mankind New Warrior Project and creator of men's empowerment groups, he has honed skills as a personal development facilitator and community builder.

In addition to his qualifications as a professional wilderness guide, certified Tantra educator and group facilitator, Robert brings 35 years of success in the corporate world as a marketing executive and multi-craft technician. He is also the father of a daughter in her thirties.

A compassionate and gifted communicator, Robert approaches people with deep respect and intuitive wisdom. He has developed an uncommon ability to create a safe, sacred space supporting profound transformation for individuals, respectful of their unique personal paths and pace of growth.

For a full listing of Robert's credentials, visit
**www.wildsacredness.com**

The exercises contained within this booklet are a precursor to the Sacred Vision Quest experience. To appreciate the impact of this profound adventure, take a moment and read what men and women are saying about Wild Sacredness and their wilderness journeys.

*"What I discovered on my vision quest is that 'out there' is really 'in here.' The process was really a soul excavation, where I was thoroughly prepared and supported by the guides to go way deep inside myself. Fear almost made me not go on the quest...but I would have missed out on the rebirthing of my life!"*

~ LORNA C., DIRECTOR – LOS ANGELES, CA

*"I got my mojo back, my joie d' vivre. I had lost my passion for life. I regained the joy of being alive."*

~ BOB K., FATHER – SUNNYVALE, CA

*"I got my self-love back on the vision quest, and I hadn't had it for 22 years. This was 'my miracle,' and it has saved my life. Now my outlook is bright; I see only good things ahead. Before I could only live day to day. My perspective on work and everything in my life has completely changed."*

~ MARK K., TRAINING COORDINATOR –
BURLINGTON, ONTARIO CANADA

*"This vision quest allowed my mind to quiet down so I could hear my own inner guidance about issues in my life. I was able to release things that were holding me back, and that process is ongoing. Letting go of old baggage and negative thoughts has made me much more powerful. This unique setting gives you the chance to find out who you really are."*

~ PEGGY T., STAFF ACCOUNTANT – OMAHA, NE

*"The experience for me was a genuine transition from one life phase to another. It was a transition into true adulthood. I'm finally able to stand behind and own my dreams."*

~ ERIC M., MUSICIAN – SAN FRANCISCO, CA

*"I reclaimed part of myself on the quest. As a result, my life is becoming more in tune with who I really am and I'm able to express my authenticity. When I returned, I made a huge change in my work situation, getting rid of something that was holding back my progress and creativity—and it brought immediate success. I'm much happier and feel richer inside."*

~ JORIS N., TRAINER/COACH –THE HAGUE, NETHERLANDS

*"Robert was an amazing guide—his demeanor is grounded, clear, generous. It was incredibly meaningful to me that he took my experience seriously; it was clear he was focusing on what I wanted for myself. He believes in the process of the vision quest totally, and he puts himself into it with full passion."*

~ ELIZABETH H., TV PRODUCER – NEW YORK CITY, NY

*"I would recommend this experience as a rare opportunity to connect with yourself and your genuineness. We're always looking for answers outside ourselves, but this quest reminds you that the answers lie within, and have always been there."*

~ TOM G., ENTREPRENEUR
CALGARY, ALBERTA CANADA

*"This is by far the most powerful, intimate process I've ever done. It went deep, and reconnected me to my true passionate self. It gave me the opportunity to share my deep, dark secrets and then go out and live with them alone in nature. I was exposed to myself, with nowhere to hide – just looking at my self, talking to it, being with it. This was worth years of therapy."*

~ CARRIE M., MOTHER – CONCORD, CA

*"I went on the quest looking to 'reset' my life – I had recently retired from work I'd been doing for decades. The quest absolutely, astoundingly reset me. It shattered my expectations. In fact, it cracked open my heart, which had not been free and open for the last 40 years. I feel like I've come out of hiding and I'm going to live my life fully from this time forward."*

~ PETER S., RETIRED – LAS VEGAS, NV

Other books by Robert E. Wagner in the Wild Sacredness Series, available at www.amazon.com (print or Kindle eBook format):

**SACRED DESIRE: *Secrets to Kindling Profound Passion***
A journey into the unlimited reservoir of erotic energy and sensual pleasure that we all possess.

**EMBRACING COMMUNITY: *Living an Inspired Life***
Takes you on one of the most intimate of all adventures—finding the purpose for your life and living it, in vibrant engagement with people you care about.

08132016

www.ingramcontent.com/pod-product-compliance
Lightning Source LLC
Chambersburg PA
CBHW060550030426
42337CB00021B/4516